SURF-FISHING BASICS

101 THINGS TO KNOW BEFORE YOU GO WITH ACCOMPANYING "FISH TAILS"

BY

BILL DOBIECKI

authorHOUSE™

1663 LIBERTY DRIVE, SUITE 200
BLOOMINGTON, INDIANA 47403
(800) 839-8640
WWW.AUTHORHOUSE.COM

© 2005 BILL DOBIECKI. All Rights Reserved.

No part of this book may be reproduced, stored in a retrieval system, or transmitted by any means without the written permission of the author.

First published by AuthorHouse 05/27/05

ISBN: 1-4208-4087-8 (e)
ISBN: 1-4208-4086-X (sc)

Library of Congress Control Number: 2005902283

Printed in the United States of America
Bloomington, Indiana

This book is printed on acid-free paper.

Co-edited by Kristina Dobiecki

INTRODUCTION

I GOT THE IDEA FOR THIS INTRODUCTION WHILE WAITING IN LINE FOR THREE AND A HALF HOURS WITH FOUR HUNDRED NINETY NINE OTHERS AT CAPE COD'S NATIONAL SEASHORE RANGER STATION, NEAR PROVINCETOWN MA. WE WERE ALL THERE FOR ONE THING, OUR OVERSAND PERMITS. THERE WAS A LIMIT PLACED ON THE NUMBER ISSUED AND THAT MADE THEM AS GOOD AS GOLD. AS THE LINE MEANDERED BACK AND FORTH WE GOT TO KNOW OUR PATIENT NEIGHBORS PRETTY WELL. WHILE MANY WERE THERE JUST TO BE ABLE TO ENJOY THE SUMMER BEACH AND SUN, THE MAJORITY OF STICKER SEEKERS WERE THERE SO THEY COULD DRIVE AND FISH THE VAST BEACH WHICH OPENS APRIL FIFTEENTH.

ALL THE STORIES I OVERHEARD AS THE LINE WOVE IN AND OUT WERE ABOUT PAST FISHING TALES, RECIPES, POLICIES, AND PLOVERS. ONE THING EVIDENT WAS THE EXCITEMENT FOR THIS YEARS FISHING SEASON. THE RECOVERY OF THE STRIPER WAS ONE REASON AS WELL AS THE KNOWLEDGE THAT WHEN YOU FISH THE OCEAN, ANYTHING IS POSSIBLE. THAT "ANYTHING" IS WHAT IS SO INTRIGUING ABOUT SURFFISHING. THE VAST OCEANS HAVE A CERTAIN INFINITY TO THEM.

THIS IS FAR DIFFERENT THAN RIVER, STREAM, LAKE AND POND FISHING WHERE, WHAT, AND HOW BIG YOUR CATCH IS USUALLY HAS PARAMETERS.

THE OCEAN ON THE OTHER HAND HAS A CERTAIN MYSTERY AS TO WHAT YOU MIGHT CATCH ON ANY GIVEN DAY OR NIGHT. THIS IS WHAT"HOOKS" MOST SURFFISHERS." THE PEOPLE IN THAT LINE, THAT DAY, WERE "HOOKED"

IF YOU'VE NEVER FISHED THE BEACHES OR JUST NEED A REFRESHER, THIS BOOK IS FOR YOU.

GET HOOKED!

DEDICATED TO LEO, MAX, GENE, TED, AND EDDIE

CONTENTS

INTRODUCTION V

BEFORE YOU GO 1

FISHING STRATEGIES 9

ON HAND EQUIPMENT 15

READING THE WATER 17

LURE TECHNIQUES 21

BOTTOM RIGS 25

BAIT TACTICS 27

SINKER TYPES 35

ANCHORING THE BOTTOMFISHING RODS IN THE SAND 37

CASTING TECHNIQUES 41

NIGHT FISHING TACTICS 47

FISH ON! 51

ROD AND REEL MAINTENANCE 55

CONGRATULATIONS! 57

ADDENDUM "FISHING LOG" 59

SURF-FISHING BASICS

BEFORE YOU GO

1) IT'S A GOOD IDEA TO CHANGE BAIL SPRINGS EACH SEASON. THERE IS ALWAYS A POSSIBILITY OF ONE BREAKING WHILE FISHING. MOST TACKLE SHOPS HAVE REPAIR STAFF ON HAND, AND THE COST IS USUALLY INEXPENSIVE.

2) HAVE YOU HAD LURE STICKER SHOCK LATELY? IF YOU HAVEN'T, LOSING A NEW TEN DOLLAR LURE ON THE FIRST CAST WILL CURE YOU. BLUE FISH WILL HIT ANYTHING BRIGHT AND THESE HOMEMADE LURES WORK GREAT!

YOU WILL NEED:

- FIVE SECTIONS OF STAINLESS STEEL COATED TUBING FROM A PLUMBING STORE, THE KIND THAT IS USED UNDER BATHROOM SINKS.
- FORTY SPLIT RINGS
- TWENTY HOOKS (TREBLE OR SINGLE, NUMBER ONES)
- HACKSAW
- SPLIT RING PLIERS
- SHOTGUN SHOT
- GRINDING WHEEL (OPTIONAL)
- PLIERS OR VISE
- DRILL

CUT THE TUBES INTO DESIRED LENGTHS

CRIMP ONE END

DRILL HOLE

BILL DOBIECKI

ATTACH SPLIT RING

ATTACH HOOK

FILL WITH DESIRED AMOUNT OF SHOT TO ACHIEVE DESIRED WEIGHT

REPEAT PROCESS AT OTHER END MINUS THE HOOK DUH! GRIND CORNERS IF DESIRED

YOU AND A FISHING BUDDY SHOULD BE ABLE TO MAKE 15 TO 20 LURES IN A COUPLE OF HOURS. SINCE THE TUBES ARE VERY PLIABLE, TRY PUTTING A BEND IN A COUPLE OF THEM TO CREATE MORE ACTION. YOU WILL GET A LOT OF SATISFACTION FROM CATCHING FISH ON YOUR OWN LURES

3) LEARN TO TIE ALL THESE COMMONLY USED FISHING KNOTS

- A) (IMPROVED TRILENE), GOOD FOR ATTACHING LINE TO SWIVELS, LURES, HOOKS, OR SNAPS.

- B) (DOUBLE SURGEONS KNOT) WHEN YOU NEED TO MAKE A LOOP AT THE END OF A LINE.

- C) (PALOMAR KNOT) SEE A ABOVE

- D) (BLOOD KNOT) TO ATTACH TWO LINE ENDS TOGETHER

4) TO TEST A DRAG TO DETERMINE IF IT NEEDS REPAIR, A NEW DRAG WASHER OR CLEANING, HOLD THE END OF THE FISHING LINE AND

GRADUALLY LOOSEN THE DRAG. AS THE REEL STARTS TO FREE FALL TOWARDS THE GROUND. IT SHOULD DESCEND IN A STEADY DROP, NOT IN A HERKY JERKY MANNER. THIS TEST IS ALSO USEFUL WHEN PURCHASING A NEW REEL.

5) YOUR TACKLE BOX LURES SHOULD CONSIST OF:

A FEW DIFFERENT COLORS AND SIZES OF:

SWIMMING PLUGS

POPPING PLUGS

METALS

BUCKTAIL JIGS

PLASTICS

ALSO:

SINKERS, TERMINAL TACKLE, LUBE, SHARPENING STONE, AND NEEDLENOSE PLIERS

6) BEFORE EVERY FISHING TRIP, CHECK THE CERAMIC EYELETS ON YOUR RODS FOR CHIPS OR CRACKS. CERAMIC IS SHARP AND IF A BIG FISH HITS, IT WILL SNAP YOUR LINE AS SOON AS THE LINE TIGHTENS.

7) LEARNING TO GATHER YOUR OWN BAIT IS A DEFINITE PLUS. A SAND EEL RAKE IS INEXPENSIVE AND FRESH BAIT IS ALWAYS BETTER. WATCHING FISHERMEN ON CAPE COD RAKE SAND EELS AND CATCH BIG STRIPERS SOON AFTER WAS ALL IT TOOK TO CONVINCE

ME. IT WILL PAY FOR ITSELF WITH MONEY SPENT ON STOREBOUGHT BAIT OVER TIME. YOU WILL NEED A BUCKET WITH A FLOAT ATTACHED BY A ROPE TO YOUR WAIST. AT LOW TIDE DRAG THE RAKE TOWARDS YOU IN THE SAND AS YOU STAND AT WAIST HIGH WATER LEVEL. THE SANDEELS GET STUCK BETWEEN THE TINES. SIMPLY DROP THEM IN THE BUCKET.

8) EXAMINE YOUR HOOKS AND TERMINAL TACKLE OFTEN. RUST AND SALT WATER CORROSION AFFECT METAL QUICKLY AND NATURAL AIR OXIDATION DULLS HOOKPOINTS. KEEP A FILE OR STONE IN YOUR TACKLE BAG AND SHARPEN BEFORE EVERY USE IF POSSIBLE. IN THE OFF-SEASON, CHANGE OR SHARPEN THEM AS NEEDED. A ROTARY TOOL WITH A STONE BIT WORKS WELL. THIS IS A GOOD MID-WINTER HOT-STOVE ACTIVITY TO PREPARE FOR THE NEXT FISHING SEASON.

9) ASK QUESTIONS WHENEVER AND WHEREVER YOU CAN. IF YOU'RE GOING ON VACATION, CALLING LOCAL BAITSHOPS IS A GREAT PLACE TO START. THERE ARE ALSO GREAT WEBSITES AVAILABLE TO BROWSE. ACCORDING TO THE SPECIFIC GAMEFISH AVAILABLE AND THE LOCATION YOU ARE

10) IN NEW ENGLAND WATERS, SHOREFISHING WILL ENABLE YOU TO CATCH THE FOLLOWING SPECIES. OF COURSE, A LOT DEPENDS ON THE LOCATION, TIME OF YEAR, TIME OF DAY, EQUIPMENT AND LUCK. LEARN TO IDENTIFY THEM BEFORE YOU GO.

SURF-FISHING BASICS

- STRIPED BASS
- BLUEFISH
- FLUKE
- FLOUNDER
- BLACKFISH (TAUTOG)
- WEAKFISH (SQUETEAGUE) (SEA RUN TROUT)
- BONITO TUNA
- FALSE ALBACORE

11) SKATES ARE OFTEN CAUGHT WHILE BOTTOM FISHING. WHILE THESE PREHISTORIC LOOKING FISH AREN'T THOUGHT OF AS GAME FISH, SOME SAVVY FISHERMEN USE A COOKIE CUTTER AND CUT "POOR MAN'S SCALLOPS" FROM LARGER SKATE WINGS. ANOTHER FISHERMEN'S TREAT ARE THE CHEEKS OF LARGE BLUEFISH. THESE"MEDALLIONS ARE MORE TENDER AND TASTY THAN THE REST OF THE FISH.

12) IF YOU LOSE FISHING EQUIPMENT DURING ANY TRIP, MAKE SURE YOU REPLACE IT ASAP. YOU WILL WANT A COMPLETE SURF BAG OR BUCKET EACH TIME YOU GO

13) REFER TO A TIDE CHART BEFORE YOU GO. IT IS AN INVALUABLE TOOL WHEN PLANNING A FISHING TRIP. MOST FISH WILL FEED WHEN THE TIDE IS MOVING IN OR OUT AND NOT AS OFTEN DURING SLACK TIDES. TWO HOURS BEFORE HIGH AND LOW TIDE ARE GOOD TIMES TO BE FISHING. IF THAT CORRESPONDS WITH DAYBREAK OR NIGHTFALL, GREAT! NOTE: WHEN FISHING BREACHWAYS (ROCK JETTYS WHICH ALLOW WATER BACK AND FORTH INTO BACK PONDS) THE TIDE CHART WILL NEED TO BE ADJUSTED

PLUS OR MINUS THE TIME IT TAKES THE POND TO FILL OR EMPTY.

14) A SIMPLE FISHING CADDY CAN BE CONSTRUCTED USING A FIVE-GALLON BUCKET. SIMPLY CARVE OUT V'S ALONG THE TOP EDGE EVERY COUPLE OF INCHES AND HANG YOUR LURE HOOKS IN THE V'S WITH THE LURES ON THE INSIDE. OTHER GEAR CAN BE PLACED ON THE BOTTOM AND COMFORTABLE SEATS CAN BE PURCHASED WHICH FIT RIGHT ON TOP OF THE BUCKET. THIS IS ESPECIALLY GOOD FOR JETTY FISHING. A BUNGEE CORD ON THE OUTSIDE OF THE BUCKET WILL KEEP THE LURES STABLE DURING TRANSPORT.

15) SURFFISHING BAGS ALLOW YOU TO PACK JUST ENOUGH GEAR FOR LONG WALKS ON JETTYS AND BEACHES. THEY CAN BE BOUGHT OR MADE. A SIMPLE CONSRUCTION CONSISTS OF ONE LITER SODA BOTTLES CUT OFF THE NECK THAT WILL HOLD LURES. DUCT TAPE THEM IN TWO ROWS OF FOUR, FIND A SUITABLE BAG WITH SHOULDER STRAP AND SOME POCKETS AND YOUR ALL SET.

16) CRIMP DOWN THE BARBS OF YOUR HOOKS WITH NEEDLENOSE PLIERS, ESPECIALLY ON TREBLE HOOKS. IT WILL SAVE TIME WHEN HOOKS NEED TO BE REMOVED AND YOU WANT TO GET THE LURE BACK IN THE WATER.

FISH "TAILS"

1984

MY FRIEND CARL AND I HAD JUST HOOKED INTO SOME BRUISER BLUEFISH JUST OUTSIDE THE PUBLIC BEACH AREA OF RACE POINT. BECAUSE WE WERE SO CLOSE TO THE SUNBATHERS, WE SOON ATTRACTED A CROWD OF CURIOUS ONLOOKERS.

I WAS USING A THREE OUNCE LEADHEAD JIG AND WAS PLAYING A FIFTEEN POUNDER FOR QUITE SOME TIME WHEN IT FINALLY BEGAN TO TIRE AND WAS COMING CLOSE TO SHORE. KEEPING MY LINE TIGHT AND MOVING BACK AND FORTH WITH THE EBB AND FLOW OF THE WAVES, THE FISH FINALLY SHOWED ITSELF. THE ONLY PROBLEM WAS THAT THE FISH SAW ME TOO! WITH ONE LAST SHAKE OF IT'S HEAD IT THREW THE TIGHT LINED JIG OUT OF IT'S MOUTH.

THE JIG FLEW BACK, WHIZZED BY MY HEAD, AND STRUCK A POOR GUY STANDING A FEW FEET BEHIND ME, RIGHT SQUARE IN THE FOREHEAD."OUCH".

WHAT MADE MATTERS WORSE IS THAT HE WAS HOLDING HIS FIVE YEAR OLD SON BY THE HAND AT THE TIME. WHEN HE CAME TO ABOUT A MINUTE LATER HE GOT UP, AND HE AND HIS SON MEANDERED BACK TO HIS BLANKET TO GET SOME ICE FOR THE RESULTING WELT ON HIS HEAD.

WE CONTINUED TO CATCH FISH UNTIL OURS ARMS WERE EXHAUSTED.

FISHING STRATEGIES

17) A TEASER TIED TO YOUR SWIVEL AND BENEATH YOUR LURE WILL OFTEN CAUSE A STRIKE WHEN THE LURE ITSELF WON'T. DON'T BE AFRAID TO TRY IT. THE TEASERS ARE AVAILABLE AT MOST TACKLE SHOPS.

18) MARK THE LEGAL LENGTH FOR STRIPED BASS OF THE STATE YOU'RE IN ON YOUR FISHING ROD. A NARROW STRIP OF TAPE PLACED THE PROPER DISTANCE FROM THE BUTT WILL DO THE TRICK. IT WILL BE A QUICK REFERENCE GUIDE SO YOU CAN RESUME FISHING QUICKLY.

19) USE CIRCLE HOOKS WHENEVER POSSIBLE. MANY CHARTER CAPTAINS CLAIM THEY ARE THE BEST. THE HOOK DESIGN CAUSES IT TO TURN AND REVOLVE TO SET IN THE CORNER OF THE FISH'S MOUTH. THIS RESULTS IN NATURAL "HOOKSETS" AND HOPEFULLY A GREATER HOOKUP PERCENTAGE.

20) MOST OF THE RODS TODAY ARE MADE OF GRAPHITE. THEY ARE STRONGER AND MORE SENSITIVE UNDER MOST CONDITIONS. HOWEVER, IF YOU PLAN ON FISHING OFF ROCKS OR JETTIES, FIBERGLASS RODS MAY BE MORE DURABLE. THEY TEND TO HOLD UP BETTER AGAINST NICKS THAT MIGHT OCCUR IF THE ROD FALLS ONTO SHARP ROCKS.

21) ALWAYS FISH WITH AT LEAST TWO RODS RIGGED. ONE SHOULD BE RIGGED FOR BOTTOM FISHING AND BE IN THE WATER AS MUCH AS POSSIBLE. THE OTHER RIGGED FOR CASTING WITH AN

APPROPRIATE ARTIFICIAL. WHETHER YOU FEEL LIKE CASTING OR THE FISH START BREAKING THE SURFACE, YOU WILL BE READY FOR BOTH STYLES OF FISHING.

22) WHEN FISHING FOR STRIPERS AND A SCHOOL OF BLUEFISH PASSES BY, WAIT AND CAST YOUR OFFERING BEHIND THE BLUES BASS OFTEN FOLLOW BLUES AND FEAST ON THE SCRAPS THE BLUES LEAVE BEHIND. BLUES ARE "CHOPPERS". THEY WILL BITE A FISH IN HALF AND GO ON TO CHASE THE NEXT ONE. THIS LEAVES SCRAPS BEHIND THAT THE BASS AND BIRDS READILY FEAST UPON. STRIPED BASS ARE "GULPERS". THEY WILL GLADLY EAT THE REMAINING SCRAPS THAT THE BLUES AND BIRDS LEAVE BEHIND. BECAUSE BLUEFISH ARE ALWAYS IN MOTION, THEIR MUSCULAR MEAT TENDS TO BE OILY, GREY AND VERY STRONG TASTING.IF YOU CATCH BLUEFISH,AND ARE PLANNING A FISH FRY ,THE BEST TASTING BLUEFISH ARE IN THE FIVE POUND RANGE, AND SHOULD BE EATEN AS SOON AS POSSSIBLE AFTER THEY ARE CAUGHT. AS BLUEFISH GROW LARGER, THEY DEVELOP A LATERAL LINE THAT MOST DINERS DESCRIBE AS "BITTER". ON THE OTHER HAND, WHEN STRIPED BASS IS COOKED, IT IS WHITE AND FLAKY AND VERY WELL RECEIVED AMONG FISHLOVING CONNOUSIERRS.

23) KEEP YOUR FINGERS ON YOUR HAND! BLUEFISH WILL BITE YOUR FINGER OFF AT ANY JOINT WITH ONE OF THEIR REFLEX JAW CONTRACTIONS. CARRY A BLUEFISH BY THE BASE OF THE TAIL, AWAY FROM BODY PARTS, AND ALWAYS USE NEEDLENOSE PLIERS TO REMOVE HOOKS FROM A LARGE BLUEFISH'S GRASP. I USE SINGLE

HOOKS TO MAKE HOOK REMOVAL EASIER. IN ADDITION; BLUEFISH HAVE AN ENZYME ON THEIR TEETH THAT KEEPS HUMAN BLOOD FROM COAGULATING AS QUICKLY AS USUAL. THESE RISKS JUST ADD TO THE FUN OF THE EXPERIENCE.

24) MOST WEEDS CAN BE REMOVED FROM YOUR LINE BY SHAKING THE ROD TIP. ONE KIND OF WEED IS (MUNG) WHICH IS REFERRED TO AS "MONKEY FUR". IT GETS ITS NAME BECAUSE IT FEELS JUST LIKE WET MONKEY FUR TO THE TOUCH. (I GUESS THE PERSON WHO NAMED THIS MUST HAVE HAD A WET MONKEY IN THE HOUSE). FORGET TRYING TO TEAR THESE WEEDS OFF. CUT THE LINE. NEAR THE SWIVEL, PUSH THE WEEDS OFF AND RETIE. YOU WILL SAVE A LOT OF TIME AND FRUSTRATION.

25) IF YOUR LURE / HOOK GETS SNAGGED ON ROCKS OR WEEDS, TRY TO SHAKE IT FREE. IF IT BECOMES APPARANT THAT IT WON'T COME FREE, WRAP THE LINE AROUND THE REEL HANDLE, TIGHTEN THE DRAG COMPLETELY AND WALK BACKWARDS POINTING THE ROD TIP AT THE LURE UNTIL THE LINE OR LURE GIVES UP ITS HOLD. THIS WILL PUT THE PRESSURE ON THE LINE AND OFF THE TIP OF YOUR ROD. NEVER YANK THE ROD SIDE TO SIDE VIOLENTLY. THIS CAN WEAKEN OR EVEN SNAP YOUR ROD. IF YOU ARE LUCKY ENOUGH TO GET THE LURE/HOOK FREE, MAKE SURE TO CHECK THE LINE FOR FRAYS.

26) IF YOU ARE TAKING A BREAK FROM CASTING, SECURE YOUR LURE. DON'T LEAVE IT DANGLING SO A PASSING HUMAN GETS HOOKED. IF SECURING IT TO THE ROD, PLACE IN THE EYE

SUPPORT AND NOT IN THE EYE ITSELF. PLACING IT IN THE EYE COULD SCRATCH THE CERAMIC AND CAUSE PREMATURE LINE FAILURE

27) WHENEVER YOU ARE FISHING ROCK JETTYS, BEWARE OF THE BLACK COATING ON THE ROCKS. WHEN IT BECOMES WET, IT'S AS SLIPPERY AS ICE.

28) IF POSSIBLE, KEEP LIGHT TACKLE HANDY. IF SMALL BAITFISH LIKE HERRING, MULLET OR SNAPPER BLUES ARE AROUND, TRY TO CATCH THEM AND USE THEM FOR LIVE LINING.

29) EARLY IN THE STRIPER SEASON, AND EVEN BEYOND, BUCKTAIL JIGS WITH PLASTIC GRUBS ATTACHED TO THE HOOK ARE VERY POPULAR WITH THE SCHOOLIES AND THEIR BIGGER BROTHERS AND SISTERS.

30) TIE A BELT AROUND YOUR WADERS ABOUT CHEST HIGH. THIS COULD SAVE YOUR LIFE IF YOU LOSE YOUR FOOTING AND FALL IN. MANY DROWNINGS OCCUR TO FISHERMEN WHO DON'T TAKE THIS PRECAUTION. NEOPRENE WADERS, WHILE MORE EXPENSIVE THAN RUBBER, FIT TIGHTER AND ARE GENERALLY SAFER.

31) STEEL LEADERS ARE NECESSARY WHEN BLUE FISH ARE IN. THEIR TEETH COULD CUT THROUGH ANY MONOFILIMENT LINE. 18 TO 24 INCHES IS A CHOICE.

32) IF PEOPLE AROUND YOU ARE CATCHING FISH AND YOU AREN'T, TRY TO SEE WHAT THEY ARE USING. THE SIZE AND COLOR COULD BE

DIFFERENT THAN WHAT YOU ARE USING AND A SIMPLE SWITCH WILL OFTEN DO THE TRICK

33) IF YOU'RE GOING ON A BEACH EXCURSION WITH THE FAMILY, FISHING GEAR SHOULD BE THE FIRST STUFF OUT AND THE LAST STUFF IN. AND WATCH OUT FOR THOSE ROD TIPS WHEN YOU CLOSE THE TRUNK! IF YOU DO HAPPEN TO BREAK OFF A ROD TIP, DON'T THROW THE ROD AWAY. PUT A NEW TIP ON THE ROD AND USE IT FOR BLACKFISH. THEY MUST BE KEPT OUT OF THE ROCKS AS SOON AS THEY ARE HOOKED AND THE STIFFER TIP OF A BROKEN TIPPED ROD WORKS REAL WELL.

FISH "TAILS"

1988

THE "DOGDAYS OF SUMMER" WERE UPON US THIS EARLY AUGUST DAY NEAR HATCH'S HARBOR. THE TEMPERATURE WAS IN THE NINETIES AND PEOPLE WERE LITERALLY BURNING THE BOTTOMS OF THEIR FEET WHENEVER THEY STEPPED ON SUN-EXPOSED SAND. EVEN THE DREADED GREENHEAD FLIES WERE SEEKING COVER UNDER OUR TARP CANOPIES. IT WAS EVEN TOO HOT FOR THEM TO BITE. THE FISH WEREN'T BITING EITHER. THE WATER AND WIND WERE DEAD CALM. SEAFARERS CALL THIS CONDITION THE DOLDRUMS AND IT WENT ON FOR DAYS.

ALL OF A SUDDEN, GOOD FRIEND ROSALIA EMERGES FROM THE WATER WITH A BLUEFISH BY THE TAIL. NO-POLE-NO BAIT –NO NOTHING BUT HER BLUEFISH. AFTER MANY JOKES ABOUT HOW SHE MAY HAVE TRAPPED SAID FISH, WE SURMISED THAT THE FISH MAY HAVE BEEN WOUNDED IN A BATTLE AND WAS WALLOWING NEAR SHORE. IT WAS PRETTY LIGHT FOR ITS LENGTH. WE STILL LAUGH ABOUT THAT ONE TO THIS DAY.

SURF-FISHING BASICS

ON HAND EQUIPMENT

34) IF YOU ARE USING TWO PIECE RODS, BUNGEE CORDS, OR VELCRO STRIPS WILL HELP KEEP THEM TOGETHER WHEN TRANSPORTING THEM TO YOUR FISHING SITE

35) KEEP PLENTY OF FRESH CLEAN WATER AVAILABLE WHEN FISHING. IT WILL PROVE INVALUABLE IF YOUR REEL FALLS INTO THE SAND OR YOU'RE FILLETTING ANY CAUGHT FISH. PORTABLE CAMPING SHOWERS WORK WELL. THEY HOLD FIVE GALLONS AND HAVE A HANDY ON/OFF SHOWER SPOUT.

36) KEEP A GAFF HANDY WHEN FISHING JETTY'S. YOU WILL NEED IT TO LAND A FISH AND AVOID SERIOUS INJURY TO YOURSELF. THE LONGER THE GAFF THE BETTER.BE SURE THE TIP OF THE GAFF HAS A PROTECTIVE SHEATH TO AVOID INJURY

37) A COMPLETE FIRST AID KIT SHOULD ACCOMPANY EVERY FISHING TRIP. THESE KITS ARE INEXPENSIVE AND INVALUABLE.

38) BAIT KNIVES(SHORTER) AND FILLET KNIVES (LONGER AND THINNER)--SHARPENED

FISH "TAILS"

1995

I HAD DECIDED TO FISH ALL NIGHT AND CHOSE THE SOFT SIDE OF CHARLESTOWN BREACHWAY. I WAS STAYING NEARBY AND KNEW THE AREA VERY WELL. AFTER GETTING SET UP AT THE END OF THE ROCKS, NIGHT FELL QUICKLY. A NEW MOON RESULTED IN A VERY DARK NIGHT AND AS THE NIGHT PROGRESSED, I WAS TREATED TO MANY SHOOTING STARS. ABOUT TWO IN THE MORNING I BEGAN TO SEE LIGHTNING FLASHES FAR BEYOND BLOCK ISLAND. THE FLASHES WERE LIKE GRAND FINALES OF FIREWORKS ON THE FOURTH OF JULYS PAST. IT TOOK A COUPLE OF HOURS FOR THE STORM TO REACH BLOCK, ABOUT ELEVEN MILES AWAY. I DECIDED TO HEAD BACK TO THE TRUCK PARKED ON THE SAND AT THE END OF THE JETTY. FIGURING IT WOULD BE A GOOD TIME TO GET A LITTLE SHUTEYE AND RIDE OUT THE STORM, I DID JUST THAT. WHEN I AWOKE THE STORM HAD PASSED AND THE SUN WAS JUST STARTING TO RISE. I EMERGED FROM THE TRUCK TO FIND FOUR SETS OF DEER TRACKS EMBEDDED IN THE WET SAND.

APPARENTLY THEY WERE CURIOUS AND WANTED A CLOSER LOOK INTO THE TRUCK. THERE ARE MANY DEER THAT INHABIT NINIGRET WILDLIFE PRESERVE. THIS IS A PROTECTED AREA BETWEEN THE BREACHWAY AND EAST BEACH.

SURF-FISHING BASICS

READING THE WATER

39) AT SOME BEACHES, LOW TIDE WILL REVEAL UNDERWATER TROUGHS THESE OFTEN HAVE ONE ENTRANCE. REFERENCE THESE SPOTS AND CAST YOUR BAIT TO THOSE OPENINGS BEFORE THE TIDE CHANGES. YOUR OFFERING WILL BE THERE WAITING FOR THE FISH TO ENTER. ALSO BE ON THE LOOKOUT FOR OTHER NATURAL TIDAL FORMATIONS SUCH AS BOWLS, POINTS, AND BARS. THESE AREAS OFTEN ATTRACT FISH.

40) WATCH AND READ THE BIRDS AND WATER. DIVING BIRDS SIGNAL THE PRESCENCE OF SCHOOLS OF BAITFISH.THESE BIRDS (TERNS AND GULLS) HOVER AND WAIT UNTIL GAMEFISH ATTACK THE SCHOOL. THIS SENDS THEM SCURREYING TOWARDS THE SURFACE OR THE SHORELINE. THE MANY BAITFISH ARE TRAPPED AGAINST THE SKY OR SHALLOW SHORELINE FOR EASY EATING. WATCH FOR THE TELLTALE "BOILS"(WHEN THE BAITFISH HAVE NO ESCAPE AND THE WATER LOOKS LIKE IT'S BOILING DUE TO THE FEEDING FRENZY) CAST OVER THE BOIL AND REEL BACK THROUGH THE FRENZY AND HOLD ON. IF YOU DON'T GET AN IMMEDIATE HIT, DON'T GIVE UP. MANY FISH WILL TRAIL THE LURE AND HIT NEAR SHORE.

41) THERE IS A SAYING IN THE NORTHEAST, "**IF THE WIND IS FROM THE WEST, THE FISHING'S BEST. IF IT'S FROM THE EAST, THE FISHING'S LEAST**".THIS REFERS TO WINDS THAT BLOW BAITFISH TOWARDS SHORE OR AWAY FROM SHORE. WHEN IT SEEMS YOU CAN CAST A MILE,

THE BAITFISH ARE ALSO STRUGGLING TO STAY CLOSE TO SHORE. WHEN YOU ARE CASTING INTO A STRONG WIND, THE BAITFISH ARE ALSO FIGHTING THAT SAME WIND. THE BAITFISH ARE MORE APT TO BE CLOSER TO SHORE. THEY ARE EASIER PREY FOR GAMEFISH AND FISHERMEN ALIKE.

FISH "TAILS

1994

I WAS FISHING WITH FRIENDS. PETE, JOHN, AND ROD BY THE WALL AT WATCH HILL'S EAST BEACH IN EARLY OCTOBER. WE ALL HAD OUR BOTTOM RIGS IN THE WATER AND WERE ANXIOUSLY AWAITING SOME SERIOUS ACTION.

THE MIGRATION WAS ON AND THE FISH WERE VERY ACTIVE PATROLLING THE BEACH BACK AND FORTH IN SEARCH OF BAIT. THEY NEED TO FILL THEIR TANKS FOR THE LONG YEARLY MIGRATION SOUTH. LOW TIDE WAS OCCURING WHICH KEPT A CONSTANT PULL ON OUR WEIGHTED LINES. IT WOULD BE EASY TO DETECT A HIT AS THE RODS WOULD BEND OVER IN SUCCESSION. WHAT HAPPENED NEXT WASN'T WHAT WE EXPECTED. INSTEAD OF OUR RODS JOLTING DOWN, THE LINES ALL WENT LIMP, IN ORDER, LEFT TO RIGHT LIKE MALE ENHANCEMENT DOSES HAD JUST RUN THEIR COURSE. WE WERE ALL CUT OFF AND FIGURED THAT A LARGE SCHOOL OF BLUEFISH SWAM BY AND CUT OUR LINES WITH THEIR DORSAL FINS. WE RE- RIGGED AND BEGAN THE PROCESS ALL OVER AGAIN.

SURF-FISHING BASICS

LURE TECHNIQUES

42) FISHING FROM OR NEAR JETTYS OFTEN PROVIDES THE GREATEST CHANCE OF FISHING SUCCESS. THIS IS ESPECIALLY TRUE IN THE SUMMER MONTHS WHEN FISH AREN'T FEEDING RAVENOUSLY IN PREARATION FOR THEIR SOUTHERLY MIGRATION. THESE JETTYS ARE MAN MADE SRTUCTURES WHICH ALLOW WATER AND BOAT TRAFFIC TO PASS BACK AND FORTH INTO BACK PONDS WITH THE CHANGE OF TIDES. THEY ARE USUALLY CONSTRUCTED OF HUGE CHUNKS OF ROCK AND EXTEND OUT FARTHER THAN ANY CASTS COULD REACH. THESE ROCKS ATTRACT BAITFISH THAT USE THEM FOR SAFETY. THIS IN TURN ATTRACTS THE GAMEFISH THAT FEED ON THEM, ESPECIALLY ON THE OUTGOING TIDE WHEN THEY SIT AND WAIT FOR THE BAIT TO TUMBLE BY.

43) AS PREVIOUSLY MENTIONED, THE BEST TIME TO FISH THESE JETTYS IS ON THE OUTGOING TIDE.

STANDING AS CLOSE TO THE END AS POSSIBLE USE A FLOATING SWIMMING PLUG OR LIVE EEL, CAST IT OUT INTO THE CURRENT AND LEAVE YOUR BAIL OPEN. THE CURRENT WILL CARRY YOUR LURE FARTHER THAN YOU COULD CAST, ESPECIALLY IF THE WIND IS BLOWING IN.EVENTUALLY THE LINE WILL EXIT THE CURRENT. WHEN IT DOES, SIMPLY START YOUR RETRIEVE AS SLOWLY AS YOU CAN AND WAIT FOR A STRIKE.

OFTEN TIMES THERE ARE OTHER PEOPLE WHO WISH TO FISH THE SAME WAY. IF THERE ARE, A CIRCULAR ROTATION USUALLY TAKES PLACE. THE CASTER MOVES TO THE OUTSIDE AND AWAY FROM THE CURRENT

AFTER CASTING TO RETIEVE THE BAIT AS THE NEXT CASTER MOVES TO THE INSIDE AND CASTS INTO THE CURRENT. SEVERAL PEOPLE CAN TAKE ADVANTAGE OF THE CURRENT THIS WAY. ON OCCASION HOWEVER, YOU WILL ALWAYS HAVE A CHANCE OF RUNNING INTO THE BUFFOON WHO THINKS THE JETTY BELONGS TO HIM.

44) STRIPERS ARE USUALLY METAL LEADER SHY, TRY USING A LENGTH OF MONOFILAMENT SHOCK LEADER (30 LB TEST) TIED DIRECTLY TO THE LURE USING A RAPALA KNOT. TIE YOUR SWIVEL 12 TO 16 INCHES FROM THE LURE AND THEN TO ANOTHER SWIVEL ATTACHED TO THE MAIN LINE. THE RAPALA KNOT ALLOWS THE LURE MORE FREEDOM OF MOVEMENT AND A MORE NATURAL PRESENTATION THAN OTHER KNOTS. YOU CAN ALSO PLACE A BARREL SINKER ON THE MAIN LINE ABOVE THE SWIVEL TO CAST SOFT PLASTICS FARTHER.

45) MAKE YOUR PLASTIC LURES WEEDLESS BY BURYING THE HOOKPOINT INTO THE PLASTIC. TRY TO PLACE THE POINT DIRECTLY ON TOP OR BOTTOM OF THE PLASTIC LURE TO PREVENT THE LURE FROM SPIRALING THROUGH THE WATER.

46) A PLASTIC JIG THREADED ON TO THE HOOK OF A BUCKTAIL ADDS ACTION AND MAKES AN ATTRACTIVE OFFERING FOR GAMEFISH ESPECIALLY STRIPERS AND FLUKE

47) AN EELSKIN RIG WORK WELL WHEN YOU DON'T HAVE THE REAL THING OR THE BAIT IS DEAD. THE JIGHEAD FOR THIS RIG USUALLY HAS A HOLE IN THE MIDDLE SO WATER CAN FLOW THROUGH AND MAKE THE LURES ACTION LIFELIKE. IT ALSO HAS A TRAILER HOOK THAT PROJECTS

DOWN THROUGH THE SKIN. YOU CAN USE A REAL SKIN AND ATTACH THE JIGHEAD WITH THREAD FOR THE BEST RESULTS.WHILE THIS IS NOT NECESSARILY A BEGINNERS TACTIC, THE SOONER YOU LEARN IT THE BETTER.

BILL DOBIECKI

FISH "TAILS"

1984

WHILE STAYING IN EASTHAM ON A FAMILY VACATION, I DECIDED TO TAKE A RIDE TO MARCONI BEACH WHICH IS PART OF THE CAPE COD NATIONAL SEASHORE. IT WAS JUST BEFORE DARK AND THE SUNBATHERS WERE LONG GONE. I WAS INSPECTING THE WATER WITH BINOCULARS IN SEARCH OF TELLTALE SPLASHES OR BIRDS DIVING WHEN A CAR PULLED RIGHT NEXT TO ME. INSIDE THE VEHICLE WAS A MAN DRIVING AND A WOMAN RIDING SHOTGUN WITH A MAP ACROSS HER LAP. SHE ROLLED DOWN THE WINDOW AND ASKED ME "CAN YOU TELL US HOW TO GET TO CAPE COD?"

BOTTOM RIGS

48) FISHFINDER RIGS ARE A FAVORITE CHOICE WHEN FISHING THE BOTTOM. WHEN A FISH TAKES THE BAIT THE LINE SLIDES THROUGH THE TEFLON SLEEVE WITH THE SINKER ATTACHED. THE FISH DON'T DETECT THE WEIGHT OF THE SINKER AND RUN UNTIL YOU SET THE HOOK. THEY ARE RELATIVELY INEXPENSIVE, EFFECTIVE AND AVAILABLE AT MOST TACKLE SHOPS. CAPE COD FISHERMEN PREFER THE "TOP AND BOTTOM" TYPE RIG. THIS RIG HAS THE SINKER AT THE BOTTOM WITH TWO HOOKS SUSPENDED AT DIFFERENT LEVELS ABOVE THAT SINKER.

ANOTHER OPTION IS A SINKER SLIDE. THEY WORK THE SAME AS A FISHFINDER RIG AND SOME FISHERMEN FIND THEM EASIER TO DEAL WITH.

49) IN ORDER TO KEEP FROM LOSING YOUR CHUNK BAIT TO CRABS, A RIG WITH AN ADJUSTABLE FLOAT WILL HELP KEEP YOUR BAIT OFF THE BOTTOM AND AWAY FROM A CRAB'S REACH.

50) BLACKFISH RIGS HAVE A SINGLE HOOK WHICH SITS NEAR THE SINKER AND CLOSE TO THE BOTTOM WHERE THE BLACKFISH LURK.

FISH "TAILS"

1979

READING THE MORNING PAPER WITH CO-WOKERS, THE TOPIC OF BLUEFISH ATTACKS CAME UP. THE ARTICLE REPORTED THAT BLUEFISH WERE ATTACKING BATHERS AND THE FISH WERE APPARENTLY ATTACTED BY SHINY JEWELRY THE SWIMMERS WERE WEARING.
THIS LED TO FURTHER DISCUSSION ABOUT BLUEFISH TEETH AND THE DAMAGE THEY CAN INFLICT.
ONE WOMAN ASKED ME WHERE I CATCH THESE TOOTHY DENIZENS. I REPLIED"RHODE ISLAND".
SHE INTURN RETORTED"THANK GOODNESS, I GO TO THE BEACHES IN CONNECTICUT"

SURF-FISHING BASICS

BAIT TACTICS

51) NEVER LEAVE YOUR BAIT EXPOSED AND UNATTENDED. IF YOU ARE MOVING DOWN THE BEACH WHILE CASTING, HUNGRY SEAGULLS WILL ENJOY THE SNACK AND YOU WILL SOON BE BAITLESS.

52) MATCH THE SIZE OF THE LURE OR CUT OF BAIT TO THE SIZE OF THE FISH YOU ARE TRYING TO CATCH. GENERAL RULE, *LARGE FISH -LARGE BAIT, SMALL FISH-SMALL*

53) LIVE BAIT IS ALWAYS BEST.IF THAT IS NOT POSSIBLE KEEP YOUR BAIT AS FRESH AND FROZEN AS POSSIBLE IN A SMALL COOLER NEAR YOUR BAITROD, THIS WILL SAVE YOU STEPS AND TIME.

54) DON'T HESITATE TO USE THE HEAD OF YOUR CUT BAIT FIRST. MANY LARGE STRIPERS HAVE BEEN TAKEN WITH THAT PRESENTATION.

55) WEARING DISPOSABLE GLOVES TO BAIT HOOKS WILL KEEP HUMAN AND OTHER CHEMICAL SCENTS OFF YOUR BAIT. THESE SCENTS CAN MAKE A STRIPER TURN AND RUN.

56) WHENEVER POSSIBLE, CHECK THE STOMACH CONTENTS OF A PREVIOUSLY CAUGHT FISH. THIS WILL HELP DETERMINE THE SIZE OF THE LURES TO USE OR HOW BIG TO CUT BAIT STRIPS. TRY TO MATCH THE SIZE FOR BEST RESULTS

57) IF YOUR'E FISHING FROM A JETTY, PULLING A WEIGHTED TREBLE HOOK QUICKLY AND

FORCEFULLY THROUGH THE WATER. MAY SNAG ANY AVAILABLE LIVE BAIT. HOOK THE LIVE BAIT AND TOSS IT INTO THE CURRRENT. LIVE BAIT IS ALWAYS BEST.

58) FISHING WITH LIVE EELS? (STRIPER CANDY), KEEP THEM FRESH AND MOIST IN A COOLER. PREFROZEN ICEPACKS WILL WORK WELL. IT'S EASY TO HANDLE A SLIMY EEL BY DROPPING IT IN THE SAND BEFORE HOOKING IT OR GRABBING IT WITH A RAG. HOOK IT UNDER THE MOUTH AND THROUGH AN EYE SOCKET. RETRIEVE VERY SLOWLY IF YOU ARE ATRUE BEGINNER, THERE ARE RUBBER EEL LOOK-A- LIKES THAT ARE VERY EFFECTIVE AND DON'T REQUIRE THE EFFORT OF LIVE EELS.

59) SAND WORMS (ALSO KNOWN AS BLOODWORMS) MAKES GREAT BAIT FOR STRIPERS .THEY CAN BE TRICKY TO RIG BECAUSE OF THE PINCERS THAT CONTRACT EVERY TIME THE WORM UNDULATES. SOME FISHERMEN CUT THE HEADS OFF BUT THE FIRM HEAD HELPS HOLD THE BAIT ON THE HOOK WHEN CASTING. GRIP THE WORM BELOW THE HEAD WITH ONE HAND AND HAVE THE HOOK READY IN THE OTHER. WHEN THE WORM OPENS HIS MOUTH AND THE PINCERS ARE EXPOSED, FORCE THE HOOKPOINT DOWN THE WORM'S GULLET. THREAD THE HOOK DOWN ABOUT A HALF INCH AND OUT THE BODY. USE MORE OF A LOB CAST INSTEAD OF A POWER CAST SO THE WORM'S BODY DOESN'T SNAP OFF.

60) SANDWORMS ALSO WORK WELL FOR TAUTOG, ALSO KNOWN AS BLACKFISH. YOU DON'T NEED THE WHOLE WORM SO CUT IT OFF AFTER

SURF-FISHING BASICS

COVERING THE SHANK AND USE THE REST LATER. YOUR BAIT WILL LAST LONGER.

61) FISH FOR TAUTOG AROUND ROCKS AND JETTY'S WITH WORMS OR GREEN CRABS. IF YOU FIND ONE, THERE ARE PROBABLY MORE.

62) GET YOUR OWN GREEN CRABS FOR BLACKFISH FROM A JETTY. TIE A CHICKEN BONE, PIECE OF SQUID, OR A HOT DOG CHUNK TO A FISHING LINE OR STRING WITH A SMALL SINKER ATTACHED TO IT. DANGLE THE BAIT BETWEEN ROCKS AND WATCH THE CRABS COME OUT TO INVESTIGATE. WHEN THEY GRAB HOLD, LIFT THE CRAB OUT OF THE WATER AND INTO A BUCKET. THIS IS A GREAT KID'S ACTIVITY WHEN THE BEACH GETS BORING.

63) TO HOOK THE CRABS EASILY, REMOVE THE PINCER CLAWS AND THREAD THE HOOK THROUGH THE NOW EXISTING HOLES IN THE SHELL. IF THE CRABS ARE LARGE, CUT THEM IN HALF FROM FRONT TO BACK.

64) IF THE CRABS ARE PLENTIFUL, MAKE A CHUM BAG. PLACE EIGHT TO TEN OF THEM IN AN ONION BAG WITH A ROCK FOR WEIGHT AND CRUSH THE CRABS. TOSS THE WEIGHTED BAG TIED TO A NYLON ROPE OUT IN THE OCEAN. THESE PARTICLES WILL ATTRACT STRIPERS AS WELL AS BLACKFISH

65) HOOKING CHUNK BAIT PROPERLY WILL INCREASE YOUR CHANCES OF SUCCESS

EELS---- HOOK THE EEL UNDER THE JAW AND OUT ONE EYESOCKET. HOLDING ON TO THE EEL WITH

A RAG OR GLOVE WILL MAKE THE TASK EASIER. IF DON'T HAVE A RAG OR GLOVE, ROLL THE EEL IN THE SAND FIRST.

BLOODWORMS---- THEY HAVE TWO PINCERS ON EACH SIDE OF THEIR MOUTH   THEY COME TOGETHER EACH TIME THE BODY CONTRACTS. THEY WILL PINCH YOU GOOD! GRASP THE WORM FIRMLY ON EACH SIDE OF THE MOUTH WITH THUMB AND FOREFINGER. WHEN THE MOUTH OPENS AND THE PINCERS ARE EXPOSED, INSERT THE POINT OF THE HOOK INTO THE MOUTH AND THREAD IT DOWN AND OUT THE BODY. THE HEAD PART IS HARDER THAN THE REST OF THE BODY AND WILL HELP KEEP THE BAIT ON WHEN CASTING. DON'T CUT THE HEAD OFF.

WHOLE FISH, (CUT UP) -----------CUT YOUR FISH ACROSS THE BODY. A WHOLE MACKERAL FOR EXAMPLE SHOULD YIELD FIVE OR SIX GOOD PIECES OF BAIT. RUN THE HOOKTIP THROUGH ONE SIDE OF THE BODY AND OUT THE OTHER SIDE. TURN THE HOOK AND REINSERT THE POINT OF THE HOOK INTO THE FLESH OF THE BAIT IN A FIRM AREA. BE SURE TO USE THE HEAD. SOME OF THE LARGEST STRIPERS HAVE BEEN CAUGHT THIS WAY.

SQUID------ TRY TO FIND SMALL SQUID THAT CAN BE HOOKED WHOLE. PULL OUT THE CENTER BODY PARTS. THREAD THE HOOK BACK AND FORTH THROUGH THE BODY TUBE AND INSERT HOOK TIP IN A FIRM MEATY AREA. KEEP THE HEAD ON. LARGER SQUID CAN BE CUT INTO FISH LOOKALIKE STRIPS AND THREADED ON YOUR HOOK

FLUKE------- CAN BE CAUGHT FROM THE BEACH AS WELL AS JETTIES. FLUKE RIGS ARE AVAILABLE AT THE LOCAL TACKLE SHOPS. STRIPS OF SQUID WHICH FLUTTER LIKE INJURED BAITFISH ARE KILLERS. FLUKE PREFER SANDY

SURF-FISHING BASICS

BOTTOMS AS THEY LIKE TO COVER THEMSELVES IN THE SAND AND AMBUSH PREY AS THEY SWIM OVERHEAD. CASTING TO SANDY UNDERWATER AREAS IS KEY.

SANDEELS----SANDEELS AREN'T EELS AT ALL BUT FISH THAT LOOK LIKE EELS BECAUSE THEY'RE SO THIN. HOOK THEM RIGHT BEHIND THE ANAL HOLE AND THEN BURY THE HOOK TIP RIGHT IN FRONT OF THE TAIL. IF TOU HAVE SMALL SANDEELS, HOOKING THEM THROUGH THE EYES MAY WORK FOR YOU AS WELL.

BILL DOBIECKI

FISH "TAILS"

1989

I DECIDED TO TAKE MY FOUR YEAR OLD DAUGHTER KRISTINA TO THE BEACH AS PART OF A CAMPING TRIP TO RHODE ISLAND. WE WERE STAYING AT BURLINGAME CAMPGROUNDS AND EAST BEACH, WHICH I HAD AN OVERSAND STICKER FOR, WAS NEARBY. WE RAN INTO A FRIEND LINDA AND HER BOYFRIEND ON THE BEACH AND SETUP CLOSE TO EACH OTHER. AS THE SUNNY DAY PROGRESSED LINDA'S FRIEND WAS FLOATING ON AN INFLATABLE WITH A MASK ON, LOOKING DOWN INTO THE WATER.

I HAD A CHUNK OF MACKERAL ON MY EVER-PRESENT BOTTOM RIG WITH NOT MUCH SUCCESS TO THAT POINT. ALL OF A SUDDEN, LINDA'S FRIEND YELLED OUT "BIG STRI". BEFORE HE COULD GET "PERS" OUT OF HIS MOUTH MY ROD WAS ON THE SAND HEADING FOR BLOCK ISLAND. (SEE CHAPTER ON ANCHORING RODS IN THE SAND) I BARELY GOT TO IT BEFORE IT WAS GONE. WHILE BLOWING THE SAND OUT AS FAST AS I COULD, I SET THE HOOK AND STARTED REELING. I COULD TELL THERE WAS A BIG FISH ON AND SOON BEGAN TO ATTRACT A CROWD OF ONLOOKERS.

THE FISH HAD A HEAD START ON ME, THE DRAG WAS WHINNING AND SHE HAD THE LINE OVER HER SHOULDER HEADING FOR DEEP WATER.

THEN SOMETHING WEIRD HAPPENED. THE LINE STOPPED GOING OUT.

WHEN I TRIED TO REEL IN, I COULD ONLY GAIN A FEW FEET. I KNEW THE FISH WAS STILL ON BECAUSE IT IN TURN WOULD ONLY TAKE A FEW FEETBACK. THIS WENT ON FOR FIFTY MINUTES WHEN FINALLY THE LINE WENT LIMP. I COULDN'T BELIEVE OR EXPLAIN WHAT HAPPENED.

THE MYSTERY WAS SOLVED A FEW WEEKS LATER WHEN

SURF-FISHING BASICS

I RETURNED TO THE SAME BEACH. AN ATLANTIC STORM HAD WASHED A LARGE TELEPHONE POLE ASHORE. IT WAS WAY BACK BY THE DUNES. THE FISH MUST HAVE WEDGED THE LINE UNDER THE POLE IN ITS SEARCH FOR STRUCTURE AND WE JUST PLAYED TUG-O-WAR UNTIL THE LINE FAILED. I CAN'T THINK OF ANY OTHER EXPLAINATION.

SINKER TYPES

66) **PYRAMID SINKERS--** ARE GOOD IN SANDY SITUATIONS BECAUSE THEY DIG IN WELL. THEY ARE NOT RECCOMMENDED AROUND ROCKS. THE CORNERS OF THE SINKERS CATCH AND HOLD WHILE RETRIEVING TOO EASILY RESULTING IN TACKLE LOSS.

67) **DISC SINKERS** --ARE GOOD AROUND THE ROCKS BECAUSE THEY ARE NARROW AND EASIER TO WORK FREE.

68) **EGG SINKERS** ARE GOOD WHEN PLACED BEFORE A SWIVEL TO CAST PLASTIC OR OTHER LIGHTER BAITS, ESPECIALLY INTO THE WIND OR TO DESCEND THE LURE INTO DEEPER WATER.

FISH "TAILS"

1994

WHILE FISHING/RELAXING ON EAST BEACH ONE SUMMER DAY, WE HEARD THE SPUTTERING OF AN OUTBOARD IN THE DISTANCE. EVENTUALLY THE SPUTTERING STOPPED COMPLETELY AND A FISHERMAN AND HIS POWERLESS BOAT WERE DRIFTING RIGHT TOWARDS US. HE THREW A ROPE TO ME AND I WAS ABLE TO PULL HIM ONTO THE SAND. THERE WAS A MILE WALK BACK TO A PHONE AND THE BOATER WENT BACK TO CALL FOR A RIDE.
THE TIDE WAS COMING IN AT THE TIME AND THE SURF WAS MODERATELY LARGE. WHEN HE RETURNED THREE HOURS LATER, HIS BOAT WAS GONE. WE WATCHED AS THE WAVES BATTERED HIS FIBERGLASS BOAT TO PIECES, LITERALLY CHOPPING IT UP AND BURYING THE PIECES AND THE MOTOR COMPLEY OUT OF SIGHT.
I GAINED A NEW RESPECT FOR THE POWER OF THE OCEAN THAT DAY.

SURF-FISHING BASICS

ANCHORING THE BOTTOMFISHING RODS IN THE SAND

69) ALWAYS ANCHOR YOUR SAND SPIKE AT AN ANGLE TOWARDS THE OCEAN. IF A FISH HITS, THE MIDDLE OF THE ROD WILL TAKE LESS OF THE FORCE OF THE RUN, ESPECIALLY IF YOUR DRAG IS SET TOO TIGHTLY. THIS STRATEGY WILL ALSO KEEP SALTWATER AND WEEDS FROM DRIPPING ON THE FACE OF YOUR REELS.

70) TUBULAR SAND SPIKES ONLY WORK WELL IN SOFT BEACH SAND IF THEY ARE SET DEEP ENOUGH. A LARGE FISH WILL TAKE ROD, REEL AND BAIT AWAY TO THE BRINY BEFORE YOU CAN SAY"SON OF A BEACH"

71) WHEN WAVES RETURN BACK TO SHORE, THEY OFTEN LEAVE HIGH SAND PROMINENCES. BURYING YOUR SAND SPIKE AT THE TOP OF THESE HILLS WILL HELP KEEP YOUR LINE ABOVE THE WAVES

72) WHEN THE BEACH IS ROCKY, AN ALUMINUM SAND SPIKE WITH A SHARP POINT AND NARROW SHAFT IS A MUST. THESE CAN BE MADE INEXPENSIVELY WITH PVC TUBING ATOP A METAL FENCE POST, OR ANGLE IRON POINTED AT THE END, ATTACH IT WITH SOME DUCT TAPE OR HARDWARE. THE HIGHER THE LINE IS ABOVE THE BREAKING FIRST WAVE, THE BETTER. THE LINE WILL STAY OFF THE ABRASIVE SAND AND ABOVE THE FIRST WAVE. THE BREAKING FIRST

WAVE CRASHING ON YOUR LINE WILL BRING YOUR BAIT CLOSER AND CLOSER TO SHORE.

FISH "TAILS"

1972

MY FIRST YEAR SURFFISHING I WAS SUPPOSED TO MEET MY FRIEND PAUL AT WATCH HILL LIGHTHOUSE. HE WAS ALREADY IN RHODE ISLAND AND WE WOULD HOOKUP AT DAYBREAK. I UNDERESTIMATED THE TIME OF ARRIVAL AND GOT THERE ABOUT A HALF HOUR LATE. I SPOTTED HIS 65 MUSTANG AND HE WAS LEANING ON THE HOOD OF HIS CAR GRINNING FROM EAR TO EAR AND WITH GOOD REASON. THERE WAS A STRIPE LYING ON THE HOOD THAT STRETCHED FROM THE WINDSHIELD DOWN TO THE FRONT BUMPER .IT HAD TO PUSH FORTY POUNDS. I VOWED NEVER TO BE LATE AGAIN.

CASTING TECHNIQUES

73) NOVICE SURFCASTERS ARE EASY TO SPOT. WHEN THEY CAST, THEY LET GO OF THE ROD WITH ONE OF THEIR HANDS. THEY TRY TO STICK THE ROD OUT FARTHER AS IF IT WILL GIVE THEM MORE DISTANCE. WHEN YOU WATCH SKILLED CASTERS IT LOOKS EFFORTLESS, AND IT PRACTICALLY IS. THEY LET THE ROD DO MOST OF THE WORK. GOOD CASTS ARE A RESULT OF PROPER WEIGHT SHIFT AND TIMING BETWEEN THE TOP AND BOTTOM HANDS.

WHILE STANDING AT A 90 DEGREE ANGLE TO YOUR TARGET, EXTEND YOUR ROD BACK AWAY FROM THE WATER AND LET THE ROD TIP DROP UNTIL YOU FEEL THE WEIGHT OF WHAT YOU'RE CASTING PULL DOWN ON YOUR ROD TIP. THIS "LOADS UP" THE ROD TIP AND STARTS THE FLEX OF THE ROD IN MOTION. IT IS VERY MUCH LIKE POLE VAULTERS WHO USE THE WEIGHT OF THEIR BODIES TO EXPLODE OVER THE BAR WHEN THE POLE RELEASES.

WHEN YOU FEEL THE ROD "LOAD UP", PULL DOWN WITH YOUR BOTTOM HAND AND DRIVE YOUR TOP HAND OVER TOWARDS YOUR TARGET.

STOP THE ROD TIP ON TOUR INTENDED FLIGHT LINE. THIS WILL KEEP THE LINE FROM CONTACTING THE EYELETS AND RESULT IN EASIER LINE RELEASE.

SHIFT YOUR WEIGHT AT TIME OF RELEASE AND BE SURE TO FOLLOW THROUGH TOWARDS THE TARGET WITH YOUR BACK LEG, VERY MUCH LIKE AN OUTFIELDER THROWING A BALL TOWARDS HOME

THESE SIMPLE STEPS WILL RESULT IN GREATER DISTANCE AND MORE ACCURATE CASTS.

74) WHEN CASTING LURES WHILE TOPWATER FISHING OR TOSSING WEIGHTED CHUNKBAITS, THERE IS A DISTINCT POSSIBILITY OF A PAINFUL LINE CUT ACROSS YOUR CASTING INDEX FINGER. THIS MOST OFTEN OCCURS TO INEXPERIENCED OR INFREQUENT SURFFISHERMEN WHO HAVEN'T DEVELOPED A "CASTER'S CALLOUS". THIS CUT CAN RUIN YOUR WHOLE DAY! AN INDEX FINGER PAD SOLD AT MANY TACKLE SHOPS WILL PROTECT YOUR FINGERTIP FROM A LINE CUT. MEDICAL ADHESIVE TAPE ALSO WORKS WELL. ANOTHER ALTERNATIVE IS A RUBBER DISHWASHING GLOVE. THEY ARE CHEAP AND YOU GET FIVE PER GLOVE.

75) BAITCAST REELS ARE MADE TO DO WHAT THE NAME SAYS. A PROPER COMBINATION WILL OUTPERFORM A SPINNING OUTFIT MOST OF THE TIME BUT REQUIRE PRIOR PRACTICE. IF YOU ARE A TRUE BEGINNER, STAY WITH SPINNING TACKLE. IT WILL PERFORM WELL UNDER MOST CONDITIONS

76) USING A BAITCAST REEL? ARE YOU AFRAID OF THE DREADED BACKLASH? IN AN OPEN AREA, PULL OUT LINE FROM YOUR REEL AND MEASURE THE ANTICIPATED CASTING LENGTH OUT, PLACE TAPE ACROSS THE REST OF THE REMAINING SPOOL. THE TAPE WILL NOT ALLOW THE SPOOL TO FREEFLOW BEYOND THAT SPOT ON THE REEL. BIRDSNESTS WILL BE HELD TO A MINIMUM.

77) YOU CAN EXTEND CASTING DISTANCE BY USING THE NEW TECHNOLOGY BRAIDED FISHING LINES. THEY HAVE SMALLER DIAMETERS WHILE MAINTAINING EXCEPTIONAL LINE STRENGTH. FOR EXAMPLE; A 24 LB TEST BRAIDED LINE, WITH A DIAMETER OF AN 8 LB MONOFILAMENT LINE PAIRED WITH A 12FT GRAPHITE ROD, WILL CAST CERTAIN LURES WELL OVER 100 YARDS. MOST FISH ARE CAUGHT CLOSER TO SHORE THAN 100 YARDS OUT. THERE ARE OFTEN TIMES WHEN ONLY LONG CASTERS ARE GETTING FISH BECAUSE THAT'S WHERE THE BAIT AND FISH ARE. MATCH THIS LINE WITH AN 11 FT MEDIUM HEAVY ACTION ROD AND YOU'RE IN BUSINESS.

78) REMEMBER TO TIGHTEN YOUR DRAG BEFORE CASTING A HEAVY CHUNKBAIT AND SINKER RIG. BE SURE TO LOOSEN THE DRAG AFTER CASTING SO YOUR LINE OR ROD WON'T SNAP IF A FISH HITS. MAKE THIS ROUTINE A HABIT.— TIGHTEN DRAG---CAST----LOOSEN DRAG

79) ALWAYS KEEP THE LINE TIGHT WHEN RETIEVING THE LURE. CASTING LIGHT LURES INTO THE WIND WILL CAUSE EXCESS LINE TO LEAVE THE SPOOL LONG AFTER YOUR LURE HAS HIT THE WATER. THIS MAY CAUSE LOOPING OF THE LINE AS YOU RETRIEVE IT AND KNOTS THE NEXT TIME YOU CAST. IF THIS OCCURS, DON'T PULL ON BOTH SIDES OF THE SNARL TO CORRECT THE SITUATION. GENTLY PULL THE KNOT AT THE BASE OF THE LOOPS UNTIL THE KNOT COMES FREE. THESE ARE REALLY FUN WHEN THEY HAPPEN WHEN THE SCHOOL YOU'VE BEEN WAITING FOR GOES BY. REMEMBER--- DON'T CAST LIGHT LURES INTO THE WIND WITHOUT A BARREL SINKER

80) IF YOU ARE FISHING WITH A SPINNING ROD, AND YOU ARE HAVING TROUBLE GETTING THE TIMING DOWN, TRY PINNING THE LINE TO THE SIDE OF THE ROD WITH YOUR INDEX FINGER UNTIL YOU ARE READY TO RELEASE THE LURE. GRADUALLY MOVE THE LINE OUT TOWARDS THE FIRST JOINT OF YOUR INDEX FINGER UNTIL IT FEELS COMFORTABLE.

81) STRIPERS, LIKE THEIR FRESH WATER COUNTERPARTS, LIKE UNDERWATER STRUCTURE. CASTING TOWARDS SUBMERGED ROCKS SHOULD INCREASE YOUR CHANCE FOR SUCCESS.

82) KEEPING METAL LURES MOVING FROM THE TIME IT IMPACTS THE WATER. IN ORDER TO KEEP YOUR LURE ON TOP AT TIME OF WATER IMPACT AND RETRIEVAL, START RETRIEVING JUST BEFORE THE LURE HITS THE WATER. THIS WILL TAKE UP THE SLACK AND THE LURE WILL START RETURNING AS IT HITS THE WATER. IF GREATER DEPTH IS DESIRED, MOST METAL LURES DROP AT ABOUT A FOOT A SECOND. COUNT DOWN TO ACHIEVE DESIRED DEPTH.

83) KEEP A RELAXED ON GRIP YOUR FISHING ROD WITH YOUR NON-REELING HAND. SIMPLY LAY THE ROD ACROSS YOUR OPEN HAND AND PALM. WHEN A FISH HITS, IT'S TIME TO HOLD ON TIGHT. YOU'LL HAVE PLENTY OF STRENGTH TO CAST ALL DAY LONG.

84) PRACTICE CASTING DURING SLOW FISHING TIMES. PICK OUT A BOAT, BUOY, LOBSTER TRAP OR OTHER TARGETS .ACCURACY IS IMPORTANT ON A CROWDED BEACH. WHEN THE FISH ARE

IN. CASTING ACROSS OTHER LINES, ESPECIALLY WHEN SOMEONE HAS A FISH ON, IS A DEFINITE NO-NO. STRAIGHT AND ACCURATE CASTS ARE A MUST.

85) YOU MAY FIND A BAITRUNNER STYLE OF SPINNING REEL ADVANTAGEOUS. THIS IS A GOOD SELECTION IF ONLY ONE FISHING OUTFIT IS PRACTICAL, OR YOU WANT TO STAY AWAY FROM CONVENTIONAL REELS. BAITRUNNERS NOT ONLY ALLOW YOU TO CAST ARTIFICIALS AND BAIT EFFECTIVELY, THEY HAVE A FEATURE THAT ALLOWS LINE TO LET OUT MUCH LIKE A BAITCASTING REEL. YOU GET THE BEST OF BOTH WORLDS. PAIR THIS REEL WITH A TEN TO TWELVE FOOT MEDIUM HEAVY ACTION ROD, TWENTY POUND TEST LINE, AND YOU'RE SET FOR ACTION.

BILL DOBIECKI

FISH "TAILS"

1994

THE GULF STREAM OFTEN COMES CLOSE TO THE NEW ENGLAND SHORE DURING THE SUMMER. THIS OFTEN RESULTS IN THE CATCHING OF SOME FISH NOT USUALLY SEEN ALONG THE RHODE ISLAND SHORE. SUCH WAS THE CASE THIS SUMMER WHEN TRIGGERFISH AND NEEDLEFISH AMONG OTHER TROPICALS WERE CAUGHT BY ME AND OTHER ANGLERS FROM VARIOUS BREACHWAYS. ANOTHER BYPRODUCT OF THE WARMER WATER WAS THE BEACHING OF DEAD SEATURTLES ALONG THE RHODE ISLAND SHORELINE. THESE TURTLES WEIGHED CLOSE TO A THOUSAND POUNDS AND DIDN'T SMELL TOO GOOD FROM LYING ON THE HOT SAND AND ROTTING IN THE SUN. ANOTHER UNUSUAL FACT WAS THAT THESE TURTLES DIDN'T HAVE THEIR SHELLS. WHETHER THIS WAS NORMAL OR THEY WERE THE VICTIMS OF POACHERS STILL REMAINS A MYSTERY.

NIGHT FISHING TACTICS

86) SINCE GOOD FISHING OFTEN OCCURS AT NIGHT, PLAN FOR A WORST CASE SCENARIO BY TYING ON SWIVELS IN A DARK ROOM. THIS SKILL IS A MUST, ESPECIALLY WHEN THE FISH ARE HITTING. - TIME YOURSELF, - GOOD FISHERMEN CAN CONNECT LINE AND SWIVEL WITH AN IMPROVED TRILENE KNOT IN LESS THAN TEN

87) PURPOSELY WRAP YOUR LINE AROUND THE TIP OF YOUR LAST EYELET. REEL IN THE LINE. YOU WILL NOTICE A DIFFERENT AND DISTINCTIVE DRAG. LEARN THIS FEELING, IT HAPPENS OFTEN AND IN THE DARKAND CAN RESULT IN THAT DREADFUL "SNAP" OF YOUR LINE. WHEN YOU ARE FAMILIAR WITH THE WAY THAT FEELS, TRY THIS NEXT.---WITH THE LINE STILL WRAPPED AROUND THE ROD TIP, BRING THE ROD TIP BACK AS IF TO CAST. DO THIS REPEATEDLY. THEN DO IT WITH THE LINE NORMAL YOU SHOULD NOTICE A DIFFERENT FEEL. ONCE AGAIN THIS SKILL WILL SAVE A LOT OF TACKLE DUE TO SNAPPED LINES

88) GLOW STICKS OR SMALL CLAMPED BELLS ATTACHED TO YOUR ROD TIPS WILL ALERT YOU TO POSSIBLE HITS BY HUNGRY FISH WHEN YOU CAN'T SEE THE ROD TIP.

89) PLACE ANY AVAILABLE LIGHT (MOON, LAMPOSTS, HOUSELIGHTS) ETC BEHIND YOUR BACK SHOULDER WHEN CASTING. THIS WILL ALLOW YOU TO SEE THE OUTLINE OF YOUR LURE AGAINST THE LIGHT. IT'S EASIER TO DETECT POSSIBLE LINE-TIP TWISTS AND LET YOU KNOW HOW MUCH LINE IS BETWEEN THE LURE AND

ROD TIP. ALSO, IF YOU POSITION YOUR SELF SO THAT YOUR BAIT ROD IS BETWEEN YOU AND THE LIGHT, YOU CAN ALSO CHECK THE STATUS OF YOUR CHUNKBAIT ROD(S) AT THE SAME TIME.

90) A CLIP ON LIGHT OR HEADLAMP AT NIGHT IS INVALUABLE. IT FREES UP A HAND AND ALLOWS YOU TO GET BACK TO FISHING QUICKLY IF YOU GET A FISH OR HAVE TO RE-RIG.

91) AT NIGHT, WHEN PHOSPHORESCENTS ARE ABUNDANT IN THE SURF, THE FISHING USUALLY DROPS OFF. THE SHINE PROBABLY SPOOKS THE FISH. FISHING THE BOTTOM INSTEAD OF RETRIEVING LURES IS YOUR BEST BET FOR SUCCESS. SHOOTING STARS, APPROACHING DISTANT THUNDERSTORMS AND THE PHOSPHORESCENCE IN THE WATER ARE PHENOMENOMS THAT COUCH POTATOES NEVER EXPERIENCE. "LUCKY ARE WE SURFFISHERS "

92) DON'T SHINE PROPANE LIGHTS, HEADLIGHTS, HEADLAMPS OR OTHER BRIGHT LIGHTS DIRECTLY INTO THE WATER. STRIPERS DON'T HAVE "WINDOW SHADES" IN THEIR EYES TO ADJUST TO THE BRIGHT LIGHT. THAT IS WHY FISHING FOR STRIPERS IS BETTER AT NIGHT, EARLY MORNING AND DAYBREAK. THEY GOES DEEP IN BRIGHT LIGHT.

93) WHEN WADING OUT AT NIGHT TO MAKE A CAST, APPROACH SIDEWAYS. ONCOMING WAVES WON'T HIT YOU HEAD ON AND KNOCK YOU OFF BALANCE. YOU CAN SAFELY FEEL FOR THAT FIRST WAVE TROUGH WITH YOUR FORWARD FOOT WITH SMALL STEPS.

FISH "TAILS"

1996

THRESHER SHARKS CAN BE IDENTIFIED BY THE LARGE BANNER LIKE TAIL THEY HAVE THAT NO OTHER SHARK POSSESSES. THE ONE I CAUGHT FROM SHORE THAT SUMMER DAY WAS ALMOST THREE FEET LONG AND ATTRACTED A CROWD. MANY IN THE CROWD SHOUTED FOR ME TO "KILL IT-KILL IT". I INSTEAD TURNED IT INTO A LEARNING EXPERIENCE AND INVITED THE NEARBY CHILDREN TO FEEL THE SHARKSKIN AND RUB IT IN OPPOSITE DIRECTIONS AND NOTE THE DIFFERENCE. AFTER EVERYONE WHO WANTED TO HAD THEIR TURN, I RELEASED THE FISH BACK TO THE SEA. NOT TOO MANY PEOPLE RETURNED TO SWIM THAT DAY. OH WELL!

FISH ON!

94) SETTING THE HOOK IS AN IMPORTANT PART OF LANDING A FISH. WNEN YOU FEEL THE INITIAL HIT, REEL UP ALL SLACK AND THEN GIVE THE ROD A GOOD YANK UPWARD AND BACKWARDS. DON'T BE AFRAID TO CROSS THEIR EYES! TOO MUCH SLACK IN THE LINE, LINE STRETCH AND POOR HOOK SET CAN KEEP THE HOOK FROM PLANTING IN THE FISH'S JAW. THIS WILL MAKE IT EASIER FOR THE FISH TO SHAKE THE HOOK FREE.

95) KEEPING THE LINE TIGHT IS IMPORTANT FROM HOOKUP TO LANDING OF THE FISH. WHEN THE FISH GETS CLOSE ENOUGH TO SEE YOU, THEY WILL OFTEN TAKE A FINAL RUN, SO BE READY, AND KEEP THE LINE TIGHT AND THE ROD TIP UP.

96) WHILE FIGHTING A FISH, LOWERING THE ROD TIP TO A POINT WHERE ALL THE STRESS IS ON THE LINE AND NOT ON THE EYELETS OF THE ROD WILL EASILY SNAP THE LINE. THE EYELETS SHARE THE ABSORBTION OF THE STRESS AND FORCE THAT THE FISH GENERATES.

97) WHEN YOU GET THE FISH CLOSE TO SHORE IN THE WAVES, IT'S IMPORTANT TO WALK THE FISH BACK UP SHORE WHEN THE WAVES COMES IN. AS THE WAVES RECEDES, WALK BACK TOWARDS THE WATER WITH THE FISH. THIS WILL HELP KEEP THE LINE TIGHT. WHEN YOU CAN GET THE

FISH LANDED, GRAB IT BY THE TAIL AND BRING IT ASHORE.

FISH "TAILS"

2004

ONE OF MY FAVORITE BEACHES TO FISH IS THE BEACH IN FRONT OF HIGHLAND LIGHT IN TRURO, MA. I USUALLY MARK FISHING HOLES AT LOW TIDE BY SETTING MY ODOMETER TO 0 AT THE START OF THE BEACH AND MARKING THE HOLES SO WHEN I RETURN I CAN FIND THEM IN THE DARK WHEN THE TIDE RISES. THIS IS A BEAUTIFUL AREA WITH CLAY OOZING OUT OF THE CLIFFS. THINKING THAT NATIVE AMERICANS USED THIS SAME CLAY TO MAKE THEIR POTTERY FOR HUNDREDS OF YEARS PAST MAKES THIS PLACE EVEN MORE SPECIAL. I DIDN'T EXPECT MUCH ACTION THAT NIGHT AS SEALS WERE PLANTED EVERY THITY YARDS ACTING LIKE A FISH BLOCKADE. ONE EVEN CAME UP WITH AN EIGHT POUND SKATE AND TOYED WITH IT AND PROUDLY DISPLAYED IT TO ME LIKE A DOG WITH A BALL THAT TEASES YOU AND WON'T GIVE IT UP. IT FLOATED ON ITS BACK AND PROCEEDED TO RIP IT INTO BITESIZE PIECES. SOON THE SKATE WAS GONE.

IT IS SAID THAT MILE HIGH MT KATAHDIN IS THE FIRST PLACE IN THE US THAT GREETS THE SUN IN THE MORNING. IF THAT'S THE CASE THEN I COULDN'T HAVE BEEN FAR BEHIND. AS THE SUN ROSE THAT MORNING I WAS TREATED TO A LARGE WHALE THAT BREACHED WITH TWO THIRDS OF ITS BODY COMPLETELY OUT OF THE WATER. IT SEEMED LIKE THE RESULTING SPLASH HIT THE RISING SUN. I COULD ALMOST HEAR THE SIZZLE! THAT VISUAL IS ETCHED IN MY MIND.

ROD AND REEL MAINTENANCE

98) MAINTAINING YOUR RODS AND REELS AFTER FISHING AROUND SALTY AIR AND WATER IS IMPORTANT... BE SURE TO REMOVE SPOOLS AND HOSE INSIDE THE REEL HOUSING COMPLETELY. ALSO; BE SURE TO CLEAN THE REEL WHERE THE BAIL WIRE CLICKS OVER. IF NO HOSE IS AVAILABLE, PUT THE REEL IN A BUCKET OR EVEN IN THE TOILET (CLEAN) AND GIVE A FEW GOOD FLUSHES. THE CIRCULATING WATER WILL DO THE TRICK. BE SURE TO KEEP THE DRAG LOOSE WHEN REASSEMBLING AND KEEP IT LOOSE UNTIL YOU USE IT AGAIN. THIS IS ESPECIALLY IMPORTANT FOR WINTER STORAGE. A LIGHT COATING WITH WD-40 AND YOU'RE GOOD TO GO. ALSO CHECK YOUR LINE TO SEE IF IT NEEDS REPLACEMENT

99) ITS A GOOD IDEA TO CHANGE BAIL SPRINGS AND DRAG WASHERS EACH SEASON. THERE IS ALWAYS A POSSIBILITY OF ONE BREAKING WHILE FISHING. MOST TACKLE SHOPS HAVE REPAIR STAFF ON HAND, AND THE AND THE COST IS USUALLY INEXPENSIVE.

100) OXIDATION WILL DULL HOOKS QUICKLY. SHARPEN AND CHECK ALL TERMINAL TACKLE AND GEAR FOR RUST OR CORROSION AND MAKE NECESSARY CHANGES

FISH "TAILS"

1976

IT WAS COLUMBUS DAY WHICH SHOULD TRANSLATE INTO GREAT FISHING ACTION. NOT! THE WATER AS WELL AS THE WIND WAS DEAD CALM. AS WE WERE STREWN ON THE ROCKS AT WATCH HILL LIGHTHOUSE CATCHING SOME RAYS IT WAS APPARENT IT WOULD BE A WASTE OF TIME HOPING FOR FISH.

ALL OF A SUDDEN, AS FAR AS THE EYE COULD SEE, THE WATER EXPLODED WITH BONITO TUNA. THEY WERE PORPOISEING AND THE WATER WAS BOILING. THIS HAPPENED FOR ABOUT TEN MINUTES. THEN, ALL OF A SUDDEN, THEY WERE GONE. THAT WAS THE ONLY ACTION THAT DAY.

CONGRATULATIONS!

101) WELL TOU DID IT. YOU COMPLETED THE COURSE AND HOPEFULLY YOU WILL LAND YOUR FISH. IF YOU DO, YOU HAVE TO CELEBRATE WITH THE "FISHERMANS HANDSHAKE"

A) WET YOUR HAND AND FOREARM TO THE ELBOW AND HAVE SOMEONE ELSE DO THE SAME.

B) START SLAPPING YOUR WET FOREARMS IN AN IRREGULAR PATTERN.—THE RESULTING NOISE SOUNDS LIKE A FISH FLOPPING ON THE BOTTOM OF A BOAT AND WILL LEAVE WITNESSES GRINNING AND SHAKING THEIR HEADS.

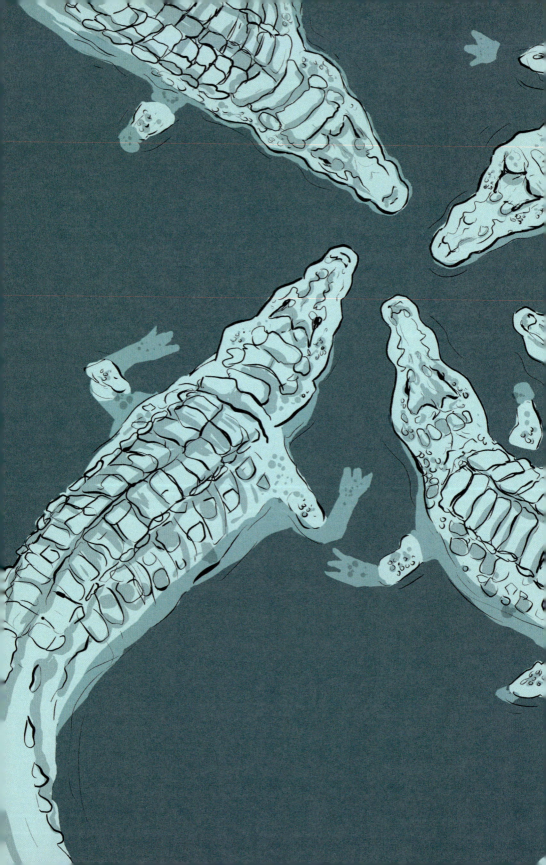

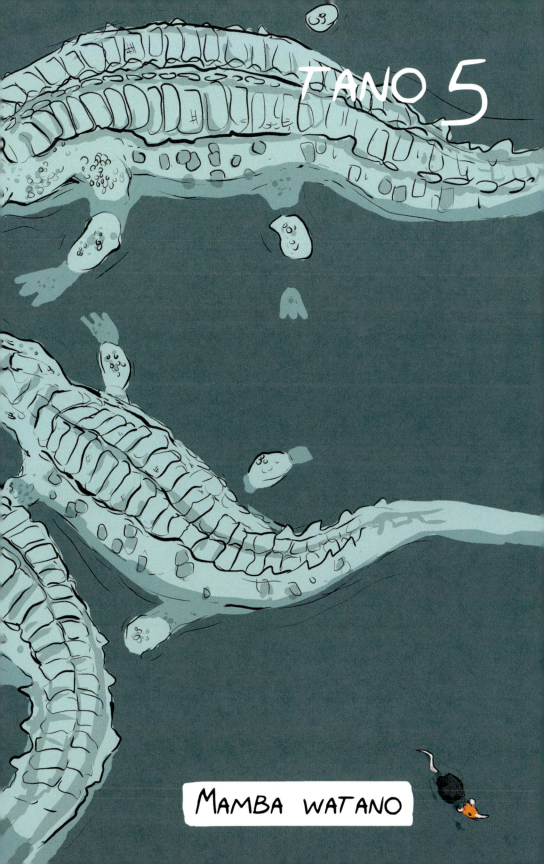

SITA 6

DIGIDIGI SITA

NANE 8

FISI WANANE

Wanyama Wa Afrika Mashariki

DIGI DIGI
Digi digi wana urefu wa inchi kumi, na uzito wa kilo sita hadi kumi na tatu. Digi digi huishi kwenye vichaka ili kujikinga na wanyama wakali. Digi digi wana aibu na hujificha mara kwa mara. Wakishituliwa hukimbia haraka wakirukaruka huku na kule na kulia "digi digi" ndio maana wanaitwa digi digi. Digi digi huishi pamoja na kutunza watoto wao. Baada ya miezi saba mama yao huwafukuza watoto kwenye makazi yao.

FISI
Fisi mwenye madoa madoa hupatikana kwa wingi katika bara la Afrika. Watoto wa fisi wakizaliwa na jinsia tofauti, hupigana sana hadi mmoja wao kufa. Fisi wa kike huishi katika ukoo na hutunza watoto wao vizuri hadi miezi kumi na mbili baada ya kuzaliwa.

KARANI
Karani ni ndege wanaopatikana Afrika nzima kusini mwa jangwa la sahara. Wana miguu mirefu inayowasaidia kuona sehemu mbalimbali juu ya nyasi wanamoishi. Tofauti na ndege wengine, karani huwinda wanyama wengine kwa chakula kwa kutumia miguu yake. Karani dume na karani jike huishi pamoja muda wao wote wa kuishi. Wakati karani dume anapotaka kukutana na karani jike, dume huruka angani na kutua chini alipo jike na kucheza kwa mabawa yao yakiwa yametanuka.

MAMBA
Mamba mwembamba mwenye pua ndefu wana umbo la wastani lenye futi kumi hadi kumi na mbili. Asili yao ni bara la Afrika na huishi kwenye maji. Wakitoka ndani ya maji, hujificha kwenye nyasi kujikinga na wanyama hatari. Mamba hutaga mayai na baada ya mtoto kuzaliwa, huanza kula na kuogelea. Muda wao wa kuishi haujulikani.

MONDO
Mondo wa Afrika ni jamii ya familia ya paka. Hupendelea kuishi wenyewe kwenye nyasi na vichaka. Huwinda chakula chao asubuhi na usiku na kwa kawaida hupumzika katikati ya mchana. Mondo hula wanyama wadogo kama panya na sengi. Mondo watoto huishi na mama yao hadi wanapofikisha umri wa mwaka mmoja na baada ya hapo mama yao huwafukuza. Mondo watoto huenda kujitafutia makazi mapya baada ya kufukuzwa na mama yao.

NYANI
Nyani huishi kwenye nyasi karibu na vyanzo vya maji, karibu na miti au kwenye kingo za mito. Nyani hupendelea kulala juu ya miti kujikinga na wanyama wakali. Watoto wa nyani hutunzwa na mama yao hadi wanapofikisha umri wa mwaka mmoja. Baba yao huwafundisha watoto vitu mbali mbali na kula pamoja nao. Nyani huishi kwenye makundi ambayo yanaundwa na nyani dume na jike.

NYUMBU
Nyumbu hupatikana mashariki mwa bara la Afrika.

Nyumbu husafiri katika makundi makubwa na hutafuta chakula chao wakati wa mchana. Nyumbu hupendelea kula majani. Nyumbu dume na nyumbu jike hukutana mara tatu katika mwaka. Nyumbu watoto hukaa karibu sana na mama yao kwa miezi kadhaa na wakati huo nyumbu dume hulinda kundi lenye nyumbu jike na watoto.

SENGI
Hawa ni wanyama wenye pua ndefu na macho madogo na hupatikana barani Afrika tu. Wamepata jina hili kwa sababu ya kuwa na pua ndefu na inayozunguka kama ile ya tembo. Sengi huishi kwenye msitu na hutengeneza njia maalumu ambazo huwasaidia kuwakimbia wanyama wakali kama nyoka.

TWIGA
Ni mnyama mrefu kuliko wote duniani. Twiga asili yao ni bara la Afrika. Twiga wanapenda nyasi kavu na kwa sababu hawanywi maji mengi, wanaweza kuishi mbali na vyanzo vya maji. Twiga ni wapole na hupendelea kuishi katika makundi ya twiga ishirini hadi thelathini. Twiga hulala wakiwa wamesimama na hulaza kichwa kwenye miguu ya nyuma.

WADUDU
Kuna aina mbali mbali ya wadudu na hupatikana katika makundi matatu. Kuna wanaozungusha kinyesi kwenye umbo la mpira na kukitumia kinyesi kama chakula. Wengine hufukia kinyesi wanachokipata. Wadudu wengine huishi ndani ya kinyesi. Wadudu huishi katika makazi mbali mbali na hupatikana kila bara duniani isipokuwa bara la antaktika.

Made in the USA
Monee, IL
16 November 2020

47947625R00017